POP! SQUIRT! SPLASH!

HANDS-ON ACTIVITIES FOR KIDS

USING SOAP, WATER, & BUBBLES

DYAN ROBSON, BLAYNE BURKE, COLLEEN BECK, MARY CATHERINE TATOY, LAURA MARSCHEL, JAIME WILLIAMS,

DEVANY LEDREW, TINA PEARSON, MELISSA LENNIG, LISETTE MARTIN, AMY SMITH, & KATIE JOINER

POP! SQUIRT! SPLASH!

HANDS-ON ACTIVITIES FOR KIDS USING SOAP, WATER, & BUBBLES

Copyright © 2015

All rights reserved.

Photography done by the respective authors.

TABLE OF CONTENTS

ART, CRAFTS, & DIY PROJECTS

BAR SOAP STAMP ART

By Colleen Beck, OTR/L · Sugar Aunts · http://www.sugaraunts.com

Did you know that you can create beautiful stamp art with bars of soap? A variety of scented and colored bar soaps can be found at dollar stores or discount stores. Cut the bars in half for an easy-to-grasp stamping tool. Use chopsticks to scrape and draw patterns in the soap. Carve lines, patterns, and dots into the cut soap bar. Pressing a tool such as a chopstick into a resistive surface, like the bar of soap, encourages hand strength of the small muscles of the hand. This activity is great for kids who are working on handwriting and pencil control. Scented soap also provides great sensory stimulation in this creative art activity. Stamp the carved bars of soap into paint and press onto paper for creative process art. You can also stamp patterns with the paint colors or soap carvings.

MATERIALS

o   Several bars of soap, cut in half

o   Chopstick

o   Paint

o   Paper

TIPS & VARIATIONS

o   Stamp soap textures into pictures and patterns.

o   Create a card or wrapping paper using the textured stamps.

o   Carve faces into the soap and discuss emotions.

o   Carve letters and numbers in the soap for more handwriting practice.

DIY STRAW BUBBLE BLOWER

By Lisette Martin · Where Imagination Grows · http://www.whereimaginationgrows.com

Blowing bubbles is one of our absolute favorite activities to do! We always have bubbles on hand because they are so easy to set up and kids of all ages love playing with them! The kids seriously never get tired of bubbles. The action of simply blowing bubbles is more than just fun. It helps children work on several developmental skills like fine motor, visual tracking, hand/eye coordination, and more. There are so many ways to turn simple objects from your home into bubble wands and these DIY straw bubble wands are no exception. We usually have straws sitting around in my kitchen utensils drawer, but we never seem to go through them, so eventually they start to take over and end up in crafts like these bubble wands. To make these DIY straw bubble blowers, we simply selected several straws from the package and used some small elastic bands to wrap both ends of the straws together. Then just dip one end of your straw blowers into your bubble solution and blow! Super easy and incredibly fun!

MATERIALS

o   Bubble solution

o   Small elastic or rubber bands

o   Straws

TIPS & VARIATIONS

o   Try blowing colored and/or scented bubbles (see pp. 10-11 for a DIY recipe).

o   Add a few drops of glycerin to your bubble mix to make larger bubbles.

o   Try different lengths and/or widths of straws.

o   Make bubble prints (see pp. 14-15) using your DIY straw bubble blower.

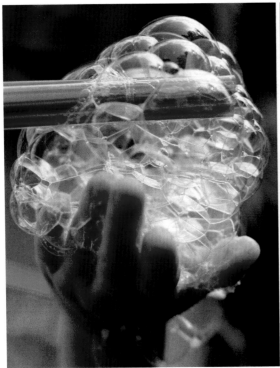 

DIY COLORED & SCENTED BUBBLES

By Dyan Robson · And Next Comes L · http://www.andnextcomesL.com

Blowing bubbles is a great boredom busting activity for kids. It also provides lots of oral motor input for sensory seeking kids, such as those with autism and/or sensory processing disorder. We like to combine calming essential oils with bubble solution as a subtle and easy way to calm kids. To make your own colored and scented bubbles, simply pour some bubble solution into a mason jar, add 2-3 drops of liquid watercolors, and 2-3 drops of essential oils. Seal the jar and shake gently until it is evenly mixed. You can substitute food extracts and even cocoa powder for the essential oils. The scents pictured from left to right above are grapefruit, mandarin orange, lemon, cedarwood, vetiver, and lavender. A majority of these essential oils were selected due to their calming and grounding properties, but they are also safe oils to use around kids.

MATERIALS

o   Bubble solution

o   Essential oils

o   Liquid watercolors (see pp. 38-39 for a DIY recipe)

o   Small mason jars

TIPS & VARIATIONS

o   Try using extracts instead of essential oils. We added a splash of vanilla extract to some bubble solution and it worked perfectly!

o   To make chocolate bubbles, add 1/2 tsp of cocoa powder to some bubble solution and mix.

o   Food coloring can be used, but caution, it may stain!

SALAD SPINNER BUBBLES

By Laura Marschel · Lalymom · http://www.Lalymom.com

Dish soap bubbles are so thick that they are almost velvety. They provide a beautiful and fun sensory experience with or without color. Add in the fun of a twirling salad spinner and you have got yourself a fun time! For this activity, simply add water and some dish soap to the bottom of your salad spinner so it just reaches the bottom of the basket. Do not add too much water as the spin mechanism is not meant to meet so much opposition and could cause your salad spinner to break. It should not cover the bottom of the basket. Put the top on the salad spinner and SPIN! Slowly, a thick froth of bubbles will form.

MATERIALS

o Dish soap

o Water

o Salad spinner

o Liquid watercolors (optional; see pp. 38-39 for a DIY recipe)

TIPS & VARIATIONS

o Try adding a drop of washable liquid watercolors or food coloring to various places and see how spinning changes it. Please note that food coloring will stain.

o Try adding a drop of cooking oil for a science experiment!

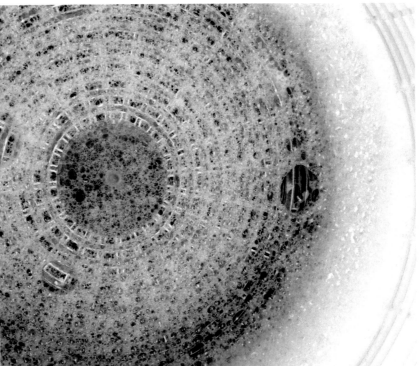

BUBBLE PRINTS

By Jaime Williams · Frogs & Snails & Puppy Dog Tail · http://www.frogsandsnailsandpuppydogtail.com

We love to try new ways to make art because trying new things with the kids is fun and exciting. I love seeing their faces light up whenever they try something new. I am a big kid at heart and have just as much fun as they do trying out these new art projects. To make the bubble paints for this art project, pour soap into the bottom of the small bowls. Add food coloring and some water. Then stir.

How to make bubble prints: Place the straw in the bubble paint bowl. Encourage your child to blow until bubbles form in the bowl. Once they have a great big bubble pile in the bowl, press the white cardstock against the bubbles.

MATERIALS

- Water
- Dish soap
- Food coloring or liquid watercolors (see pp. 38-39 for a DIY recipe)

- Small bowls
- Straws
- White cardstock or thick paper

TIPS & VARIATIONS

- Hand soap or body wash can be used instead of dish soap.

- Try using the DIY scented and colored bubbles (see pp. 10-11 for the recipe) to make bubble prints.

- Try using DIY straw bubble blowers (see pp. 8-9) or bubble snakes (see pp. 22-23) to make bubble prints art.

SOAP SHAVINGS BOOKMARKS

By Colleen Beck, OTR/L · Sugar Aunts · http://www.sugaraunts.com

This soap craft is as beautiful as it is simple. Kids will love to use a vegetable peeler on bars of soap to create soap shavings. To make the bookmarks, lay a sheet of wax paper out on a hard surface like a cookie sheet or cutting board. Peel long strips of soap and small shavings and mix the colors of the different bars of soap on the wax paper. Arrange the soap peelings on the wax paper and place the second piece of wax paper on top. Carefully move the wax paper to an ironing board. Place a dish towel over the wax paper and using an iron heated to medium, slowly press down. Check often to see if the wax paper is adhering. Cut the wax paper into rectangular bookmarks. Finish off the bookmarks by hole punching and tying a piece of ribbon.
Please note: This craft should be done under close supervision of an adult. For younger children, provide hand-over-hand assistance with the vegetable peeler. Adults may want to complete the peeling portion of this soap craft. Adults, or responsible older children, should manage the iron. As always, use judgement when it comes to completing this and any activity with your kids.

MATERIALS

- Bars of soap in several colors
- Vegetable peeler
- Two sheets of wax paper
- Iron
- Dish towel
- Hole punch
- Ribbon

TIPS & VARIATIONS

- Vary the scents and colors of your bookmarks by using various soaps.
- Add a personal message or quote to the bookmarks.
- Add flower petals or scraps of paper to the soap shaving before ironing.
- Arrange the soap shavings in a mosaic or mandala pattern.

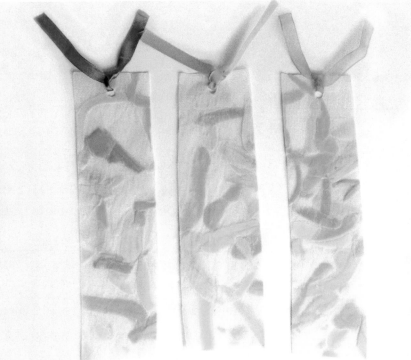

OIL & WATER PRINT ART

By Lisette Martin · Where Imagination Grows · http://www.whereimaginationgrows.com

This simple activity is color mixing, science, and art all rolled into one! Kids can make predictions about what color will result when they mix two colors together, explore the science behind why oil and water do not mix, and create a simple, but beautiful, art project. The best part is it is all done with simple materials that you likely already have on hand!

To make these prints, you will need a shallow baking dish or tray filled with a thin layer of water. We filled ours with just enough to cover the bottom of the tray. Next, let your kids use droppers to add oil and liquid watercolors and use the dropper to mix some colors around. Then when the kids are done mixing, simply place a piece of paper over the water, letting it absorb the colors and oil. Once absorbed, remove paper and let it dry.

MATERIALS

o   Water

o   Cooking oil

o   Paper

o   Eye droppers

o   Shallow baking dish or tray

o   Liquid watercolors (see pp. 38-39 for a DIY recipe) or food coloring

TIPS & VARIATIONS

o   Add drops of color to the oil after making predictions about whether it will mix or not.

o   Use color combinations that mix well together so you do not end up with brown or black.

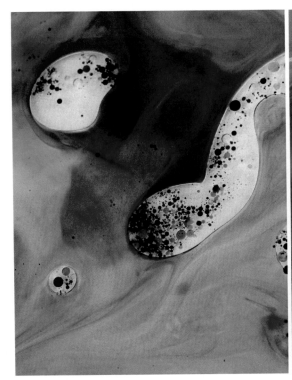

SOAP FOAM PAINTS

By Dyan Robson · And Next Comes L · http://www.andnextcomesL.com

Easy to make and even easier to clean up, these soap foam paints make great finger paints or bath paints. Because they are made with foaming hand soap and washable liquid watercolors, you can simply rinse them in the sink or down the drain after bath time. We love to use castile soap in our foaming soap dispensers because it is gentle on all skin types, but any kind of foaming hand soap will work.

To make these paints, use a foaming soap dispenser to fill the muffin tins with soap foam. Add 1-3 drops of liquid watercolors to each container of soap. Mix thoroughly with a spoon or paint brush and that is it!

MATERIALS

o   Foaming hand soap

o   Liquid watercolors (see pp. 38-39 for a DIY recipe)

o   Muffin tin or small cups

TIPS & VARIATIONS

o   Add some essential oils to make scented soap foam paints.

o   Try using soap foam paints as body paints, finger paints, bath paints, or to paint water (see pp. 34-35). The cleanup is really easy if you are already in the bathtub!

o   Food coloring can be used, but caution, it may stain!

o   Try using our chocolate soap foam recipe (see pp. 80-81 for recipe) as a paint instead.

BUBBLE SNAKES

By Melissa Lennig · Fireflies and Mud Pies · http://www.firefliesandmudpies.com

Designing bubble snakes from disposable water bottles is easy and fun! Kids will love creating long "snakes" of soap foam that can be used for sensory or imaginative play.

To make a bubble snake, simply cut the bottom off of a plastic water bottle with a serrated knife. Place the bottom half of a sock over the cutout area and secure with duct tape. Remove excess fabric with scissors. To blow bubbles, dip the sock end of the water bottle into a pan of bubbles. Blow into the bottle and see what happens!

Please note: Children who have not yet mastered blowing should refrain from participating in this activity.

MATERIALS

- o Bubble solution
- o Disposable water bottles
- o Serrated knife and scissors
- o Socks

- o Duct tape
- o A Pan

TIPS & VARIATIONS

- o Add liquid watercolors (see pp. 38-39 for a DIY recipe) to the bubbles to create rainbow soap foam!
- o Experiment with textured fabrics. What kind of fabric makes the best foam?
- o Add a scent to the bubbles (see pp. 10-11 for a DIY recipe) for oral motor input sensory seeking kids.
- o Use colored bubbles to make bubble prints (see pp. 14-15).

DISH SOAP PAINT

By Colleen Beck, OTR/L · Sugar Aunts · http://www.sugaraunts.com

Painting is a fun way for children to create and express themselves. This simple dish soap paint uses just two ingredients that combine to make bright and bold shades with a shiny finish. The paints will lose the shine as they dry, but the vivid shades remain. To make dish soap paint, pour liquid dish soap into an ice cube tray. You can use any containers, but the small compartments of an ice cube tray are perfect for holding many different shades of color. This paint really goes a long way, so a small amount of paint will last. Add a few drops of liquid food coloring to each compartment of the ice cube tray. Experiment with the amount of drops you add. More food coloring will provide a darker shade, while just one drop will give you a pale color. Your child will love dropping in the food coloring and watching as the color spreads across the dish soap. Use a toothpick for each color and carefully stir the food coloring into the dish soap to combine. Using a paintbrush, paint the colors onto paper. Clean off the brush by dipping into a cup of water and swiping excess paint and water onto a paper towel.

MATERIALS

- o Liquid dish soap
- o Food coloring
- o Paintbrush
- o Ice cube tray or small containers

- o Toothpicks
- o Paper

TIPS & VARIATIONS

- o Use the paints to fill in coloring book pages.
- o Paint pictures to music.
- o Add scented oils or extracts to add a sensory twist to painting!

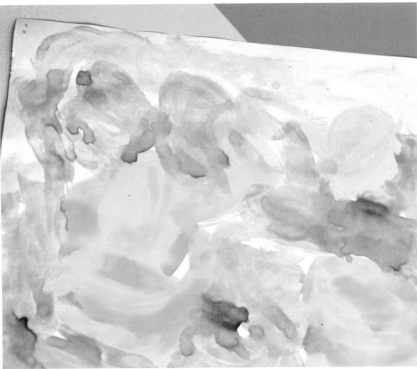

SOAP BOATS

By Melissa Lennig · Fireflies and Mud Pies · http://www.firefliesandmudpies.com

Carving soap boats from Ivory soap is entertaining and fun! Kids will get a kick out of using plastic spoons and knives to hollow out bars of soap for fine motor practice and sensory play.

To make a soap boat, remove the soap from the packaging. Show your child how to use a plastic spoon to carve the soap into a boat. Use scissors to cut a sail out of construction paper. Push a toothpick or skewer into one end of the boat and then attach the sail with a piece of tape. Float the boats in the bathtub or a plastic bin of water!

MATERIALS

- Ivory soap
- Plastic knives and spoons
- Toothpicks or wooden skewers
- Scissors

- Tape
- Plastic bin
- Water

TIPS & VARIATIONS

- Decorate the sails with stickers.
- Float the boats in different liquids like vinegar or juice and observe what happens.
- Attach the soap boats to each other with string and toothpicks to make a soap train!

JUICE BOX BOATS

By Jaime Williams · Frogs & Snails & Puppy Dog Tail · http://www.frogsandsnailsandpuppydogtail.com

The kids had some juice boxes outside during playtime one day and they left them on the deck. When I went to pick the juice boxes up, I thought that turning them into boats would be a fun idea. I decided to set up a juice box boats water bin for our next adventure outside. I had the kids save their juice boxes for the next few days until we had enough. All three of my kids had a blast playing with these boats!

To make a juice box boat, take an empty juice box and remove the straw. Cut craft foam to fit the sides and top of the juice box. Let the kids tape the foam to the "boat." Cut a foam sail and tape it to the straw. Using a knife, make a hole in the top of the box for the sail. Let the kids poke the straw through the hole to make the sail.

MATERIALS

- o Empty juice boxes
- o Craft foam sheets
- o Tape
- o Scissors
- o Water to float the finished boats on

TIPS & VARIATIONS

- o Instead of using craft foam sheets, you can leave the juice boxes plain.
- o Try decorating the juice boxes with foam stickers instead of using craft foam.

WINDOW PAINTS

By Tina Pearson · Mamas Like Me · http://www.mamaslikeme.com

Painting is a great way to develop fine motor skills and help children express their creativity. These window paints are so simple to make, use only two ingredients, and can be stored for future use. Simply grab a few empty containers (we like baby food jars for these) and mix equal parts baby soap and washable paints. Depending on how much you want to make, you can turn the paint making experience into a great measuring activity for the kids. The kids can also mix the paints to create their own colors. All of my kids, from two to nine years old, enjoy using these. They make the perfect activity for rainy days or when it is too hot to be outside. They also clean up easily leaving your windows cleaner than before you started!

MATERIALS

o   Baby soap

o   Washable paints

o   Small jars or containers

TIPS & VARIATIONS

o   Make these with scented bath wash for an extra sensory experience.

o   Use egg cartons to create a palette for your child to mix their own colors.

o   The windows clean easily with a wet rag, but if you try this activity on patio doors, try letting the kids wash them down with water guns first. It is one time they will not complain about clean up!

WATER GUN ART

By Blayne Burke · House of Burke · http://www.houseofburkeblog.com

We are always looking for new and innovative ways to paint at our house. Water guns have recently become a new obsession and are fantastic for working on fine motor skills and enhancing hand-eye coordination. Combine the two together and you have an exciting way to make art!

To start, make your water gun paint by mixing finger paint and water. Tape several pieces of paper up at your child's eye level. This activity is best done outside. Give your child the water gun filled with the color of their choice and let them begin their target practice. Do not forget to switch colors at some point. The effect of multiple watercolors on the paper is beautiful.

MATERIALS

o   Water

o   Finger paint

o   Water gun

o   White cardstock

o   Tape

TIPS & VARIATIONS

o   Once the paper is saturated, replace with a new piece and let the original dry. You do not want your child's art to become oversaturated or it may rip!

o   Use this activity as a jumping off point for a color mixing activity. Let your little one pour two colors into the water gun and see what color shoots onto the paper.

PAINTING ON WATER

By Dyan Robson · And Next Comes L · http://www.andnextcomesL.com

Once you have tried making our soap foam paint recipe (see pp. 20-21), then you will certainly want to try this colorful, tie-dye inspired activity too! Fill up a bin or shallow dish with a small amount of water. You want just enough water to cover the bottom of the container. Place generous amounts of soap foam paints on the water and start swirling the different colors together with a paint brush. Not only will the kids make some beautiful tie-dye art in the water, but they will be exploring color mixing as well.

MATERIALS

o   Soap foam paints (see pp. 20-21 for recipe)

o   Bin, tray, or dish with a tiny bit of water

o   Paint brushes

TIPS & VARIATIONS

o   Take a piece of paper and press it onto the painted water to make a cool art print (see pp. 18-19 for similar process).

o   When the kids are done painting, add corn starch to the colorful water until it turns into oobleck (usually it is one part water to one part corn starch).

o   Dip cotton balls in the painted water to make dyed cotton balls.

KITCHEN TOOLS BUBBLE WANDS

By Laura Marschel · Lalymom · http://www.Lalymom.com

Blowing bubbles is such a classic activity for kids. Nothing signifies the carefree feelings of childhood more than an airy, floating bubble. Why not try some new tools to make bubbles and see how it can add to the fun? The best part is that you can search through your kitchen cabinets to find things you already own.

Pour a thick layer of bubbles (a centimeter or so thick) into your dish or plate. Take turns dipping your kitchen tools into the bubbles and blowing bubbles! We found that the small red can strainer was the hardest to blow bubbles with. The white plastic strainer had a flat bottom so it worked fine, but you had to reload frequently. Our favorite tool was the small fine mesh sieve. Sometimes it made lots of separate tiny bubbles and sometimes it made big frothy clumps of tiny bubbles.

MATERIALS

o   Bubble solution

o   Shallow rimmed dish or plate

o   Kitchen tools such as: wire mesh sieves, plastic strainers, can strainers, splatter screens, etc.

TIPS & VARIATIONS

o   Take turns guessing which tools will be the best bubble wands. See how the different shapes (rounded versus flat), hole size, and hole spacing affect the ability to make bubbles.

o   While one person blows bubbles, another person can use their strainers and sieves to try to catch the bubbles!

o   Try using colored and/or scented bubbles (see pp. 10-11 for a DIY recipe) with these DIY wands.

DIY WATERCOLORS

By Amy Smith · Wildflower Ramblings · http://www.wildflowerramblings.com

Creativity can flow when you set out an array of paints for your children. Watercolor paints, in particular, allow your child the freedom to use long brush strokes without worrying about getting enough paint on the brush. Setting a palette of vibrant watercolor paints out for your child does not have to break your budget as you can use the ink that is stored in those dried out markers that you would normally throw away.

To make your own watercolor paints, simply separate your colored markers (reds/pinks, yellows, blues, greens) and place them, tip down, in small glass jars filled with water. You can use as little as three markers in one small jar or more to make the color darker and more vibrant. Wait at least two days. When you take your markers out of the water, you can use the same markers to begin the process again and create lighter colors.

MATERIALS

o Water

o Dried up markers (washable to prevent staining)

o Glass jars

 TIPS & VARIATIONS

o Add your favorite essential oil to your paints for a soothing effect during painting.

o Turn on some classical music to inspire your child while they paint.

o Inspire your child to create by placing flowers or an art book full of classical paintings in front of them.

o Use these DIY watercolors instead of liquid watercolors in sensory play recipes like soap foam or play dough.

MAGIC SOAP DYE ART

By Colleen Beck, OTR/L · Sugar Aunts · http://www.sugaraunts.com

This activity is a twist on the classic magic milk and dish soap experiment. To conduct the experiment, pour a small amount of milk into shallow plates or dishes. Add a few drops of liquid food coloring. Dip one end of the straw into dish soap and then slowly dab the dish soap onto the surface of the milk. Watch as the colors begin to swirl and move in the milk like magic! So what is the science behind what is happening? The molecular makeup of dish soap weakens the bonds of fat molecules in the milk. The swirling color from the food dye allows you to see the action. This experiment is fun on its own, but you can use the dyed milk and soap mixture in absorption dye art. Swirl the colors completely into the milk. Then make a few small plates with single colors of food coloring. Capture the color by carefully draping the paper towels into the plates. The colors will slowly seep across the paper towel.

MATERIALS

- Liquid dish soap
- Milk
- Food coloring
- Straw

- Paper towels
- Plates with a small lip edge

TIPS & VARIATIONS

- Explore color mixing by allowing the colors to seep into one another on the paper towel.

- Use scented dish soap for a sensory spin on this activity.

- Mix droplets of food coloring in the soap and try to capture the colors before they mix. You may end up with swirling colors on the paper towel!

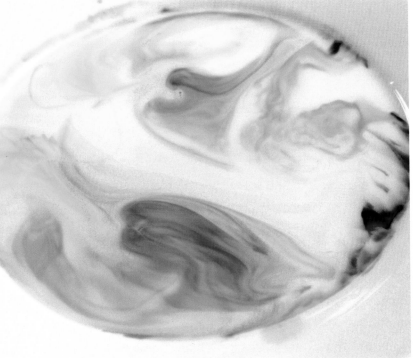

CHALK PAINTED ROCKS

By Tina Pearson · Mamas Like Me · http://www.mamaslikeme.com

This open-ended activity is great for all ages and it also lends itself to scientific exploration. Simply soak the chalk in water and find some rocks to use as your canvas. The water will soften the chalk and allow the kids to create vivid paintings on their rocks. I like using a container with multiple sections, like you can find in dollar stores, so that the kids can see what happens to the water when they soak different colored chalk in each section. As they work, we talk about how the water changes the chalk, which is great for expanding their vocabulary — is the rock rough or smooth? Is your chalk hard or soft? Which is easier to break? What happens to the paintings as the rocks dry? I also like to supply paint brushes so that the kids can paint with their chalky water. They love watching the water "magically disappear" and evaporate as it dries. In the end, we typically end up with wonderful chalk soup and some vibrant rock creations.

MATERIALS

o   Water

o   Chalk

o   Rocks

o   Paint brushes (optional)

TIPS & VARIATIONS

o   Use the chalk to draw letters or shapes on the rocks and have the kids paint over them with water to make them disappear. It is a simple way to work on letter formation!

o   Add a bucket of soapy water and make a "rock washing station" for after the kids are finished painting.

o   Try using this wet chalk painting method on other surfaces like sidewalks, black paper, etc.

SOAP FLOWERS

By Katie Joiner · Happily Ever Mom · http://www.happilyevermom.com

When I think of flowers, I always think of my daughter because she absolutely loves flowers. That is why I was thrilled to see her constructing flowers from soap shavings! It was a fun, new medium for her to play with and the soap shavings encouraged her to make 3D representations of her favorite thing on Earth. First, we shaved off the longest edge of a soap bar with a vegetable peeler. I was able to shave long, thick strands of soap, and although the shavings were much smaller and less uniform, my five year old daughter loved the chance to shave a few with my help. My daughter arranged the curled shavings into flower shapes. An easy way to extend this activity is to offer paint brushes and watercolors. My daughter crumbled a few of the shavings in order to paint them, but she also managed to paint delicately along the edges of a few shavings. While we made flowers for this activity, kids can certainly arrange them in whatever shapes they like.

MATERIALS

o   Bars of soap

o   Vegetable peeler

o   Watercolors (optional; see pp. 38-39 for a DIY recipe)

TIPS & VARIATIONS

o   If you use Ivory soap, put the soap flower in the microwave for 1-2 minutes to see it expand and change. Ask children to explain how the flower changed.

o   Put small amounts of baking soda onto each flower petal. Let kids drop vinegar onto each petal and watch their flower erupt!

o   Take the soap flowers into the bath! Kids will love using their own artwork as a way to clean up during bath time.

LEARNING ACTIVITIES & GAMES

FOAM BLOCKS MATH IN WATER

By Devany LeDrew · Still Playing School · http://www.stillplayingschool.com

What started as a simple foam shape sensory bin turned into several hands on math lessons. I love how play naturally evolves into discovery based learning! We added foam shape blocks to a bin of water. The kids immediately began to build with the blocks, but we could only balance a few on top of each other before they toppled over in the water. What else could we try? The kids sorted the blocks by shape and color. We know from other play activities that wet foam sticks together so soon they were building long rows of sorted shapes. We stuck the rows to the side of the bin like a graph. We also discussed how organizing data in this way allows us to discover quickly without counting which has the most and the least. Another variation we did was making patterns. One of us would begin a color and shape pattern before handing it off to another person to name and continue the same repetitions. We also put several blocks together using two colors to demonstrate fractions. For example, one fourth of our square is blue and three fourths is red.

MATERIALS

o   Water

o   Foam blocks

TIPS & VARIATIONS

o   This activity is perfect for math in the bath! Take the learning into the tub for inside play!

o   Instead of using a bucket or a bin of water, try using a spray bottle with water to make the blocks stick together!

SUPER SUDSY SCIENCE

By Mary Catherine Tatoy · Fun-A-Day · http://www.fun-a-day.com

Amaze young scientists with a chemical reaction made of a few household ingredients! Place a few tablespoons of baking soda into a jar or cup. Place the jar in a large container (to catch all of the suds). Pour vinegar into a measuring cup and then add some shampoo. Mix the liquid with a spoon. Invite the children to come see what happens when the vinegar-shampoo mixture is poured over the baking soda! Encourage the kids to prolong the experiment by adding more baking soda and stirring the concoction. More vinegar can be added as needed too!

MATERIALS

o   Shampoo or liquid soap

o   Vinegar

o   Baking soda

o   Mason jar or cup

TIPS & VARIATIONS

o   Add some liquid watercolors (see pp. 38-39 for a DIY recipe) or food coloring to the vinegar before starting the experiment.

o   Glitter would add some sparkle to the sudsy fun, too!

o   Try scented shampoos (coconut, apple, lavender, etc.) to engage the children's sense of smell.

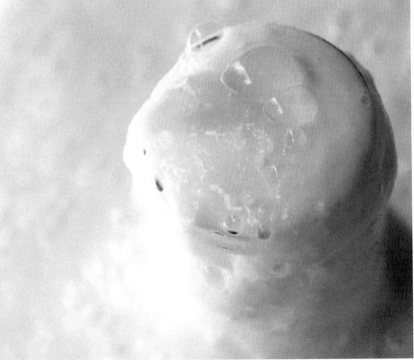

WATER POURING KITCHEN

By Amy Smith · Wildflower Ramblings · http://www.wildflowerramblings.com

Children learn many practical skills when they are trusted with tasks in the kitchen. You can create your own "kitchen" outdoors to lessen the mess inside. With just a few materials, your child can enjoy hours of playtime while learning valuable life skills! There is no need to buy new items. Simply set a small, child-sized table outside with numerous real kitchen items. It is important to honor the child with items similar to what they see adults use in the kitchen. Provide water to pour, funnel, strain, and spoon while your child explores! Your child will develop fine motor control while grasping bowls and pitchers and carefully pouring the liquid back and forth. Children learn how to self-correct when given opportunities to pour and transfer liquids. This exercise will provide confidence to your child in learning valuable daily living practices and is a step towards helping a child "do it themselves," which is a principle foundation for Montessori learning.

MATERIALS

o Water

o Table

o Bowls

o Spoons

o Colander/strainer

o Funnel

o Scoops

o Jars

 TIPS & VARIATIONS

o Color the water with food coloring to enhance the activity with color mixing exploration.

o Add your favorite essential oil to the water to enhance the sensory experience.

o Add flowers, sticks, and/or leaves to your table as "food" for your child's kitchen.

o Give your child opportunities to pour and transfer other materials such as sand, salt, beads, or rocks.

GROSS MOTOR COLOR MIXING

By Blayne Burke · House of Burke · http://www.houseofburkeblog.com

This gross motor activity involves moving the body while also engaging in color mixing. Color mixing is such a fun way to explore water while learning. For this activity, you will need two clear containers. Glass bowls work perfectly. Fill each one half way with water. Choose what end color you want to create and drop the corresponding color tabs or some food coloring into the bowls. Now here is the fun part! Encourage your little one to fill their cup halfway with one color. Then have them walk to the other bowl of water and transfer the cup of water into the bowl. Observe what color is created. After the initial water transfer, send your child back to the first bowl to fill their cup halfway again. Then have them transfer the water by other methods. Try asking them to walk sideways, skip, run, walk backwards, spin around, etc. from one bowl to the other to make the transfer! Be careful not to spill!

MATERIALS

o Water

o Two clear bowls or dishes

o A cup

o Food coloring, liquid watercolors (see pp. 38-39 for a DIY recipe), or color tabs

TIPS & VARIATIONS

o Have four bowls set up and hold races to see who can transfer the water and achieve their fully mixed color the quickest.

o Set up multiple bowls to transfer into and make several different colors at the same time using the base color. For example, set up a yellow bowl on one side and blue and red bowls on the other side to make green and orange.

MUSICAL WATER JARS

By Lisette Martin · Where Imagination Grows · http://www.whereimaginationgrows.com

Homemade musical instruments are not only fun crafts for kids, but they are also amazing ways to let children explore rhythm and sound. These musical water jars turn into a simple DIY xylophone activity that your kids will love. Even the youngest of children will have fun exploring sound with this easy project.

To make these musical water jars, you will need a few simple items from around your kitchen: mason jars and water. Have your kids help you fill each mason jar with a different amount of water. To kick it up a notch, we also added a few drops of food coloring to each jar, turning ours into a musical rainbow.

MATERIALS

o   Water

o   Mason jars or glass cups

o   Spoon or butter knife

o   Liquid watercolors (see pp. 38-39 for a DIY recipe) or food coloring (optional)

TIPS & VARIATIONS

o   Explore the difference in sounds by trying different utensils or plastic silverware.

o   Play mimicking games by tapping a series of jars and having the kids repeat.

o   Try tapping in different areas of the jar to see if it affects the sound created.

o   Compose a song with colored stickers on a piece of paper, then tap the song on the jars.

WATER & LAND ANIMAL SORTING

By Devany LeDrew · Still Playing School · http://www.stillplayingschool.com

The most versatile and well loved toys in our home are our plastic animal figures. We worked math and science into our water play by sorting animals into their habitats. Set out a bin of water next to the basket of animal toys. Then take turns choosing animals. Ask children, "What animal is this? Does it live in the water?" The animals that spend most of their time in the water go into the water bin. Splash! The land animals remain outside. Our toddler loves animals so he quickly caught on to this activity. He began sorting independently as we discussed the names of animals. He lined the land animals up outside the water bin as if they were watching the water animals in an aquarium!

MATERIALS

o   Bin of water

o   Plastic animals

TIPS & VARIATIONS

o   Add play dough for the land animals' homes! Green play dough can be grass, brown can be dirt, and white can be snow. Discuss the environments where the animals live while you sort them!

o   If you have more than one of each animal, ask your child to sort them into groups and count.

ANGRY BIRDS CUP KNOCK DOWN

By Laura Marschel · Lalymom · http://www.Lalymom.com

Knock down games are so much fun for kids. This DIY version takes the fun outside with some silly, squirty fun! It is inspired by a fun and addicting video game where you use a giant sling shot to send different birds flying into a stacked structure, trying to knock down eeeevil piggies. In our version, the birds are actually the targets. Backwards, but still fun!

To make your Angry Birds, take your red cups and add googly eyes. Cut two obtuse triangles of foam or felt (one slightly larger than the other) for each cup and glue them on as beaks. Set aside to dry. Once the cups are all dry, head outside and fill a bucket with water. Take turns stacking the birds up, loading the squirt guns and water blasters with water, and squirting them down!

MATERIALS

- Water

- Bucket

- Squirt guns, water blasters, or similar

- Red plastic cups

- Googly eyes

- Glue or hot glue gun

TIPS & VARIATIONS

- Stacking the cups alone is a lot of fun, but to extend the activity add in additional materials for building larger and more challenging structures, such as craft sticks, recyclable containers, waterproof toys, etc.

- You can also make one bird from another color and try out your target practice skills. Stack the cups and try to knock down the odd colored cup only.

- As your kids play, they may come up with their own ways to play just like mine did!

COLORED WATER DICE GAME

By Mary Catherine Tatoy · Fun-A-Day · http://www.fun-a-day.com

Add some math and fine motor skills to water play with this fun, simple game! Fill two large cups or jars with water. Color the water in one container using liquid watercolors or food coloring. Add a different color to the other jar. Set up the game by giving each player a jar of colored water, an eye dropper, a die, and a small empty cup. To play the game, player one rolls her die. She then adds the appropriate number of droppers full of colored water to her small cup. Then it is over to player two. The players continue to take turns until one of them fills up their small container.

MATERIALS

o Water

o Liquid watercolors (see pp. 38-39 for a DIY recipe) or food coloring

o Dice

o Eye droppers

o Mason Jars or cups

TIPS & VARIATIONS

o Let the kids explore color mixing after the game is over. They can mix up their colored waters and see what happens!

o Use larger droppers or small measuring cups instead of eye droppers.

o If children are working on addition, let each player have two dice. When it is their turn, they have to add the numbers on the dice together.

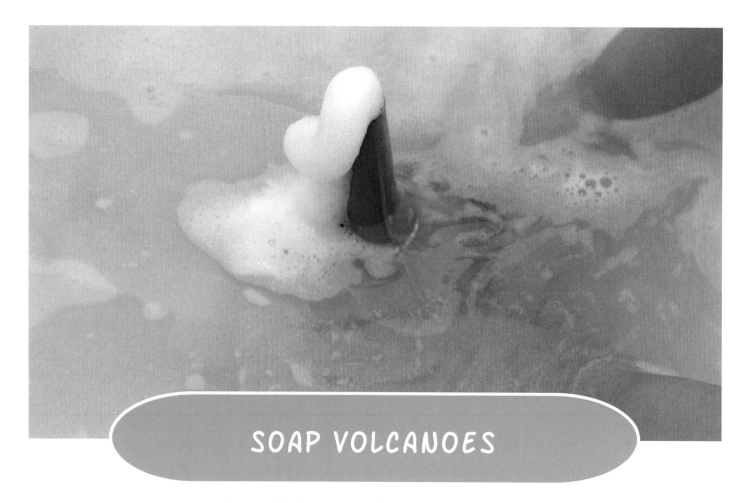

SOAP VOLCANOES

By Devany LeDrew · Still Playing School · http://www.stillplayingschool.com

Water play is a favorite in our house, but sometimes due to weather we cannot take the fun outside. This activity is the perfect indoor invitation to play with water and soap since it all it requires is a sink! Fill a funnel with foaming hand soap. Turn the funnel upside down in the sink and plug the drain. Ask your child to hold the funnel down. As the water fills the sink, it will push the soap foam up and out of the funnel. You have an instant foaming soap volcano! I am sure you will want to try this simple activity again and again! Just be sure that children are supervised so that they do not accidentally overfill the sink. You can discuss the science behind this experiment with your child by talking about how the soap foam bubbles float on the surface of the water. Can you draw a picture of what is happening inside the funnel as the water fills the sink? This super simple soap and water activity is a blast and clean up is a snap! It is a motivating way to get kids to wash their hands since all you need to add to the routine is a funnel.

 MATERIALS

o   Foaming hand soap

o   Funnel

o   Sink with a stopper or plug

 TIPS & VARIATIONS

o   Color your own homemade soap foam by mixing dish soap, a bit of water, and food coloring with your electric mixer. Use your colored bubble foam in place of the foaming hand soap!

o   Experiment with different sized funnels to see how the "volcano" transforms.

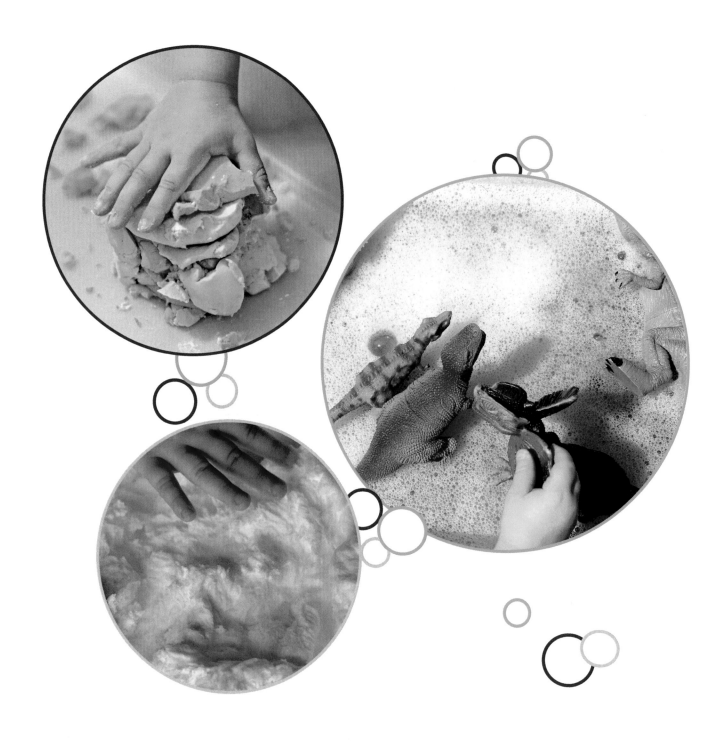

SENSORY PLAY

SOAP FOAM DOUGH

By Dyan Robson · And Next Comes L · http://www.andnextcomesL.com

This soap foam dough has quickly become a favorite of my youngest son's. It is moldable like play dough, but snaps cleanly like silly putty. It is simple to make, taking only a few minutes to prepare, and cleans up super easy since it just melts when water is added to it.

To make soap foam dough, you will need 2 cups of foaming hand soap (or make your own soap foam with liquid soap and a splash of water), 3/4 cup of cornstarch, and 1/4 tablespoon of coloring. Mix and knead the dough until it is smooth. You may need to sprinkle up to 1/2 tablespoon more cornstarch into the dough. It should not be sticky and the dough should snap in half when you put pressure on the ball of dough.

MATERIALS

o   Foaming hand soap or soap foam

o   Cornstarch

o   Liquid watercolors (see pp. 38-39 for a DIY recipe)

TIPS & VARIATIONS

o   Explore fractions by snapping the dough into equal pieces.

o   Add water to the dough and let it turn into colorful oobleck.

o   Use scented foaming hand soap or add essential oils to make scented soap foam dough.

o   Use kitchen utensils like a knife, a rolling pin, or cookie cutters while playing with this dough.

o   You can leave out the liquid watercolors to make plain white soap foam dough and make snowmen!

JELL-O SOAP FOAM

By Mary Catherine Tatoy · Fun-A-Day · http://www.fun-a-day.com

Playing with bubbles and soap foam is a blast for most kids. Take it to another level by adding Jell-O powder for color and scent. Add about 1/4 cup of water to a mixing bowl, along with about 3 tablespoons of Jell-O powder. Add about 4 tablespoons of dish soap, then mix at the highest level possible. Mix for a few minutes until the soap foam "rises" and has a thicker consistency. Transfer the soap foam to a large container and let the fun begin! Let the kids plunge their hands right into the soap foam and start playing. They might want to make designs or even handprints in the foam. Bring in some favorite toys, scoops, or measuring cups for those kids who do not want to get their hands too soapy.

MATERIALS

o   Water

o   Dish soap

o   Jell-O gelatin powder

o   Mixer

TIPS & VARIATIONS

o   We used a stand mixer to make our soap foam, but a hand mixer would work well too!

o   Add liquid watercolors (see pp. 38-39 for a DIY recipe) to make the colors even more vibrant.

o   Clear, unscented dish soap is the best bet for this activity so that the soap does not override the scent of the Jell-O.

o   Use Jell-O soap foam to make soap foam dough (see pp. 68-69 for the recipe).

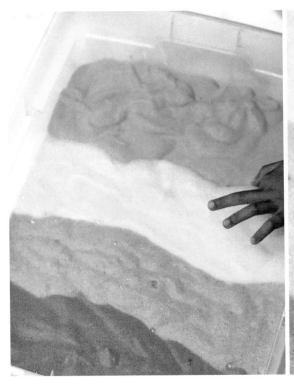

SOAP SHAVINGS SENSORY BIN

By Blayne Burke · House of Burke · http://www.houseofburkeblog.com

This soap shavings sensory bin is a fantastic way to let your little one explore the science behind bubbles while having some incredibly messy fun! To create this sensory bin, grate the soap with a grater (caution: graters are known to take chunks out of even the most confident of users, so grate safely, friend!). Once all of your soap is grated (how do those muscles feel?), set the bin out for your child with an assortment of accessories such as spoons, whisks, cups, and a squirt bottle full of water. Encourage them to explore the dry soap first. Then demonstrate how to squirt the water all over the soap. The wet soap will first turn to goo that they can explore. As they play, the saturated soap will begin to produce bubbles. The whisk is a fabulous tool for stirring up some really cool bubbles and soap foam. The true bonus is this sensory bin doubles as your child's bathtime. You are welcome!

MATERIALS

o Bars of soap

o Grater

o Squirt bottle filled with water

o Spoons, whisk, and/or cups

o Large bin or dish

TIPS & VARIATIONS

o Add some dolls or animals to the mix and encourage your little one to wash them.

o Dip bubble wands into the soap and water mixture and produce bubbles of your own!

o Try different scents and colors of soap to give your sensory bin more depth!

o Cheap soap can be found at dollar stores in bulk.

CLOUD SOUP

By Katie Joiner · Happily Ever Mom · http://www.happilyevermom.com

I love activities that are dynamic, which is why I love this simple cloud soup that starts as a science experiment and ends with fun sensory play! In order to make cloud soup, you will start with the classic Ivory soap experiment. For this experiment, you will need a bar of Ivory soap and a microwave. We cut the soap into fourths so that the "explosion" was smaller on our plates. Put one section of soap on a microwavable plate and heat for 1-2 minutes. You will see the bar of soap start to expand immediately! Make sure your kids are in a place where they can see the reaction happening inside the microwave. It is also a great time to use words like reaction, expansion, and ask children what changes they see. We extended this simple science experiment by smashing the expanded soap and adding water to make a simple cloud soup. My kids added glitter, food coloring, and small animals as more ways to extend the activity.

MATERIALS

o Ivory soap

o Water

o Spoons

o Food coloring (optional)

o Glitter (optional)

TIPS & VARIATIONS

o Before making cloud soup, use the smashed soap flakes as fake snow. Add snow animals and create a simple sensory small world!

o After the kids are done playing with the soup, add some sand to the mixture. It makes the sand moldable and dense. In fact, it reminded us of sandy cake batter! As a bonus, the sand is easily cleaned off of hands because of the soap.

PONY BEAD SENSORY SOUP

By Dyan Robson · And Next Comes L · http://www.andnextcomesL.com

Sensory soups are a great way to combine water play with real utensils from the kitchen. For a simple punch of color, I added a bucket of pony beads to the water. These little beads are perfect for scooping and pouring and older toddlers and preschoolers will love the simplicity of this colorful sensory bin. My kids loved to sort the beads by color and count while they played. So much simple learning occurred in this simple sensory bin!

Please note: Pony beads are a choking hazard. Substitute the beads with different materials to tailor it to the age and skills of your child. See the variations section for other suggestions.

MATERIALS

o   Water

o   Pony beads

o   Kitchen utensils: ladle, large spoon, whisk, measuring cups, etc.

o   Bowl

TIPS & VARIATIONS

o   Try using translucent pony beads and a glass dish or bowl on the light table.

o   Replace the pony beads with ping pong balls, glass stones, buttons, LEGO bricks, figurines, feathers, cut up straws, or any other materials that your kids might enjoy.

o   Adding measuring cups and measuring spoons are great ways to work on math skills!

SIBLING-LED WATER PLAY

By Blayne Burke · House of Burke · http://www.houseofburkeblog.com

If you have multiple kids, then you know that finding activities that they both enjoy can sometimes be a challenge. One of the ways we like to combat this issue at our house is to let our oldest child be involved in some of the decisions. Allowing your older child to set up activities for their younger siblings gives them a sense of involvement, pride, and accomplishment!

For this activity, provide your older child with a large bin filled with water. Allow them to decide on what color to make the water and help them color it. Now for the exciting part, let them choose what they would like to add to the bin based on their sibling's interests. For ours, my oldest chose rubber ducks and boats. Encourage them to be the one to introduce the water play to their younger sibling and to help them explore it. This activity is a great way to foster cooperative play and sibling bonding.

MATERIALS

o   Water

o   Food coloring, bath tabs, or liquid watercolors (see pp. 38-39 for a DIY recipe)

o   Large bin or dish

o   Fillers of your child's choosing

TIPS & VARIATIONS

o   If your younger child is old enough to reciprocate, then allow them to switch off and create a bin for their older sibling!

o   Feel free to ask questions to help your child guide their sibling in play.

CHOCOLATE SOAP FOAM

By Dyan Robson · And Next Comes L · http://www.andnextcomesL.com

Chocolate soap foam sounds and smells as decadent as you would think. And it feels silky smooth just like liquid chocolate too! We paired the cocoa powder with almond scented castile soap, which boosts the olfactory component of this sensory activity. It smelled absolutely amazing! Heavenly, even.

To make chocolate soap foam, use an electric hand mixer or stand mixer to mix a generous amount of liquid hand soap with a splash of water and a teaspoon of cocoa powder. The amount of cocoa powder you use will depend on the volume of soap foam that you are mixing. Simply mix until it is foamy and bubbly. Or read the tips section to find out how you can just use a foaming hand soap dispenser to easily make soap foam.

MATERIALS

o   Liquid hand soap

o   Water

o   Cocoa Powder

TIPS & VARIATIONS

o   Try different spices such as cinnamon or nutmeg or combine cocoa powder with scented hand soap.

o   Instead of using a hand mixer to blend the bubbles, use a foaming hand soap dispenser to quickly make soap foam. It is great fine motor work for kids!

o   Keep a towel and some water handy for easy clean up or play outside and use the hose to clean up.

o   Try turning the leftover chocolate soap foam into soap foam dough (see pp. 68-69 for the recipe).

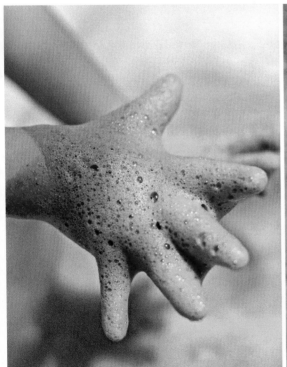

FAIRY TALE WATER BIN

By Mary Catherine Tatoy · Fun-A-Day · http://www.fun-a-day.com

This simple water play activity is perfect for a preschool fairy tale theme or just for kids who love a little extra sparkle! Have the children help fill up a bin with water, then bring out the craft jewels. Let the kids pour the jewels into the water and start exploring. Children can scoop, pour, measure, and transfer the bejeweled water as they see fit. It is easy to incorporate math into this water bin if the kids are so inclined. Encourage the children to sort the jewels by color, size, or shape. They can also count the jewels or create patterns with them.

MATERIALS

o   Water

o   Craft jewels

o   Mason jars or cups

o   Tongs or scoops

TIPS & VARIATIONS

o   Add plastic fairy tale characters to the mix for pretend play.

o   Use "magic wands" (sticks or toy wands) to stir the water with.

o   Add a bit of liquid watercolors (see pp. 38-39 for a DIY recipe) or glitter for some extra bling!

RAINBOW CLOUDS

By Tina Pearson · Mamas Like Me · http://www.mamaslikeme.com

This colorful activity combines science exploration with developing fine motor skills, and is an appealing sensory experience for all ages. Start out by microwaving a bar of Ivory soap for two minutes on a microwave-safe plate. As the soap heats, it softens and expands up to six times the size of the original bar. While the soap cools, mix each Kool-Aid packet in a separate small bowl with one cup of water. Let the kids help measure the water and practice pouring and stirring the mixture. These important preschool life-skills are so easy to incorporate into everyday activities. Transfer the soap to a shallow container and let the kids take some time poking, pinching, and testing out their "soap clouds." Use eye droppers to transfer water from the bowls onto the soap clouds. The soap absorbs the Kool-Aid creating a vibrant rainbow effect. Complete your sensory experience by having the kids squish the rainbow clouds into an awesome soapy foam!

MATERIALS

o   Ivory soap

o   Kool-Aid mix packets

o   Water

o   Eye droppers

TIPS & VARIATIONS

o   Two bars of soap fill a 9" x 13" container.

o   Remove the rotating plate from the microwave to keep the soap from hitting the edges and breaking as it expands.

o   Replace the Kool-Aid with food coloring or liquid watercolors (see pp. 38-39 for a DIY recipe).

ORANGE SENSORY SOUP

By Dyan Robson · And Next Comes L · http://www.andnextcomesL.com

Sensory soups are a great way to work on fine motor skills and explore mathematical concepts such as volume, measurement, and estimation. I personally love sensory soups because they are so easy to put together. Literally dump all the materials into a sensory bin and it is ready to go! Plus, these sensory soups are great for a variety of ages. For this orange sensory soup, we paired orange zest with some mandarin orange essential oil. It smelled absolutely divine! If you omit the essential oil, however, then this sensory soup would make a great taste-safe water play idea for babies and young toddlers. You could also try one of the variations using lemon or lime zest!

MATERIALS

- Water
- Orange zest
- 2-3 drops of mandarin orange essential oil (optional)

- Kitchen utensils: ladle, large spoon, whisk, measuring cups, etc.
- Bowl

TIPS & VARIATIONS

- Try adding slices of orange.
- Try lemon or lime zest with the corresponding essential oil.
- Add a drop of food coloring or liquid watercolors (see pp. 38-39 for a DIY recipe) to dye the water the same color as the fruit used.

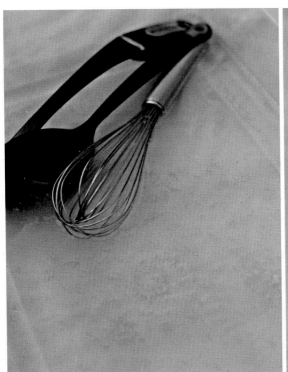

SOAP DOUGH CUPCAKE SHOP

By Mary Catherine Tatoy · Fun-A-Day · http://www.fun-a-day.com

Use soap and water to create a fun sensory and pretend play experience. Grate a few bars of Ivory soap with the children. Dip fingers into a bowl of water, adding tiny amounts of water to the soap shavings. Encourage the kids to use their fingers to mix the soap shavings and water. Doing so will form a fun sensory dough! Set out materials for the cupcake shop, then let the children start creating. They can pretend to run their own bakery—making cakes and cupcakes, decorating them, and selling them to customers. When they are done, the soap can be dried out and saved for later. Or perhaps the children would like to see what happens when it dissolves in water.

MATERIALS

- Ivory soap (or any other kind of bar soap)
- Grater
- Water
- Cupcake liners
- Utensils like an ice cream scoop (optional)
- Decorations like sequins or cut up straws (optional)

TIPS & VARIATIONS

- Use shaving cream as pretend icing for the cupcakes.
- Add liquid watercolors (see pp. 38-39 for a DIY recipe) or food coloring to the soap dough.
- If the dough is not malleable, add a little more water. If it is too soft, add in more soap shavings.
- Try using soap foam dough (see pp. 68-69 for recipe) for this activity instead.

DINOSAUR SENSORY SWAMP

By Blayne Burke · House of Burke · http://www.houseofburkeblog.com

One of our favorite simple sensory activities is adding animal figures to water. There are so many different variations and the pretend play that emerges from it is endless! One of these variations is a dinosaur sensory swamp because let's face it, what little one does not think dinosaurs are AWESOME? The best part is it is fun for all ages! Your littlest explorers can play right alongside your oldest, encouraging cooperative sibling play.

To recreate this fun sensory experience, you will need to fill a bin half way with water, add some green coloring, some baby wash (scented baby wash adds an extra sensorial experience!), and your favorite dinosaurs! The soap bubbles add a swampy feel to the green water. We also like to add some spoons and cups to broaden play scenarios.

MATERIALS

o   Water

o   Baby wash

o   Green food coloring

o   Plastic dinosaur figurines

TIPS & VARIATIONS

o   Add cloths or rags to the bin and encourage the kids to give the dinosaurs a bath.

o   Play around with different objects that correspond with your theme or add plastic trees for the dinosaurs to interact with.

o   Try jungle animals or ocean animals instead of dinosaurs.

WATER BALLOON SENSORY BIN

By Jaime Williams · Frogs & Snails & Puppy Dog Tail · http://www.frogsandsnailsandpuppydogtail.com

We love simple water play at my house. I love that it is easy for me to setup and that they have so much fun with the ideas. The water balloon sensory bin was simple, yet so much fun. My kids had a "splashing" time playing with it. To make this sensory bin, fill up a bin with water. Then add water balloons to the bin. Now let the kids play. This activity was a fun sensory experience for the kids. It is also great for multi-aged children. My oldest had just as much fun as my youngest did with this water bin. I loved seeing the little one's face when he picked up his first water balloon. And he soon caught on that after you investigated the balloon, you throw it. Ball, or balloon, throwing is great for gross motor skill development too.

MATERIALS

o   Water

o   Water balloons

TIPS & VARIATIONS

o   We use an under the bed storage bin as a water bin, but you can use a water table or large bucket too.

o   Try this activity in the bathtub instead!

o   Add colored water to the bin.

o   Add glow sticks to the water for some extra fun!

INDEX

DYAN ROBSON - AND NEXT COMES L

Dyan is the Canadian mom and part time piano teacher behind the blog *And Next Comes L*. She is married to her high school sweetheart and has two sons. Her blog focuses on autism, hyperlexia, hypernumeracy, and sensory resources.

http://www.andnextcomesL.com

JAIME WILLIAMS - FROGS AND SNAILS AND PUPPY DOG TAIL

As a mama to three high energy boys, life never slows down for Jaime, but she wouldn't have it any other way! They love creating, learning, and crafting together on *Frogs and Snails and Puppy Dog Tail* and they can easily turn anything into an adventure.

http://www.frogsandsnailsandpuppydogtail.com

LAURA MARSCHEL - LALYMOM

Laura is stay at home mom to two sweet redheads who fuel all the fun you find on *Lalymom*. Clever crafts, fun fine motor ideas, and awesome educational activities are what you will find on her blog. Come join the fun!

http://www.Lalymom.com

BLAYNE BURKE - HOUSE OF BURKE

A WAHM mom, shop owner, and blogger at *House of Burke*, Blayne has two sons: a wild ginger haired toddler and a sweet mischievous infant. Her blog focuses on crafts and activities for babies and toddlers as she prepares to homeschool her children in the future.

http://www.houseofburkeblog.com

LISETTE MARTIN - WHERE IMAGINATION GROWS

Lisette, a former preschool teacher turned work-at-home daycare provider, is the blogging mom behind *Where Imagination Grows*. Her blog focuses on play based learning activities for toddlers and preschoolers.

http://www.whereimaginationgrows.com

AMY SMITH - WILDFLOWER RAMBLINGS

Amy, M.Ed., writes about preschool and homeschooling at *Wildflower Ramblings*. As a former kindergarten teacher, she is passionate about interest-based learning and literacy.

http://www.wildflowerramblings.com

COLLEEN BECK, OTR/L - SUGAR AUNTS

Colleen, OTR/L, is the creator and head author of *Sugar Aunts*, a blog by three sisters who share creative kids activities and crafts, encouraging learning and development in everyday fun. Colleen is a mom to four and an aunt to 11. She's been an occupational therapist since 2000.

http://www.sugaraunts.com

TINA PEARSON - MAMAS LIKE ME

Tina is a former elementary school teacher turned WAHM to 4 active boys and one baby girl! She runs an in-home daycare and writes about their adventures cooking, crafting, and learning through play at her blog *Mamas Like Me*.

http://www.mamaslikeme.com

MARY CATHERINE TATOY - FUN-A-DAY!

Mary Catherine is mama to an elementary-aged boy and a preschool teacher to many. She's a licensed teacher with a specialization in early childhood education. On *Fun-A-Day*, Mary Catherine shares ideas for fun and meaningful learning activities.

http://www.fun-a-day.com

MELISSA LENNIG - FIREFLIES & MUDPIES

Melissa shares her love of nature, play, and simple crafts through her blog, *Fireflies and Mud Pies*. An educator and mom to two boys, she enjoys photography, writing, and baking.

http://www.firefliesandmudpies.com

DEVANY LEDREW - STILL PLAYING SCHOOL

Devany is a former kindergarten teacher who now homeschools her own children. She writes about how they learn through play and interest based academics at *Still Playing School*.

http://www.stillplayingschool.com

KATIE JOINER - HAPPILY EVER MOM

Katie is a happy-at-home mom. She's got a 5 year old girl and a 2 year old boy. When she's not busy saving her cats from the kids and trying to figure out what's for dinner, she can be found admiring, dreaming, and playing the day away with her family at *Happily Ever Mom*.

http://www.happilyevermom.com

27713665R00055

Made in the USA
Middletown, DE
20 December 2018